# THAT WHICH SAID

## A COLLECTION OF COMEDIANS' POETRY

# THAT WHICH IS NOT SAID

## A COLLECTION OF COMEDIANS' POETRY

Edited by Simon Pearce

Cover by David Shrigley

Illustrations by Lydia Thompson

*

a look at you publication

Published 2006 in Great Britain by
look at you productions
186a Deptford High Street * London * SE8 3PR

**Limited Edition. 1000 copies only.**

ISBN
0-9553703-0-2
978-0-9553703-0-4

Compilation © Simon Pearce look at you 2006
Cover illustration by David Shrigley
Poem illustrations by Lydia Thompson

Owen O' Neil's 'Drama in the Good Bookshop' reproduced
courtesy of Thirsty Books 2003.

All profits from this book go to the very excellent
homeless charity Crisis, www.crisis.org.uk

**www.lookatyou.info**

# CONTENTS

Foreword by Simon Munnery     9

**Tim Key**. 368.     11

**Simon Munnery**. Oh Father.     12

**Adam Buxton**. You're Getting Married.     13

**Isy Suttie**. My Dad.     14

**Robert Newman**. The Invisible Republic.     15

**Wil Hodgson**. I'm A Man.     16

**Arthur Smith**. Odd Sox.     17

**Robin Ince**. The Inanimate Are Trying To Destroy Me.     18

**Simon Bird**. Haiku.     20

**Tim Vine**. Film Poster.     21

**Mark Watson**. The Changeover.     22

**Phil Nichol**. Kill Yourself.     24

**Steve Hall**. A Poem I Sent A Girl When I Was Seventeen and Scary.     25

**Paul Foot**. Somme Mothers Do 'Ave 'Em.     26

**Andrew Maxwell**. Hello Heckler.     27

**Harry Hill**. Three Nut Poems.     28

**Tony Law**. The Sausage Inquisition.     30

**Arthur Smith.** And Drunk.                                          32

**Josie Long.** The First Time My Mum Met My                          33
Boyfriend.

**Simon Day.** The Bold Peanut.                                       34

**Simon Munnery.** Were I to be Asked Again.                          35

**Boothby Graffoe.** The Little Known Freudian                        36
Slip of Martin Luther King.

**Dan Antopolski.** These Are Three Fridge                            37
Magnet Poems I Done.

**Alex Horne.** Why some birds look pissed off.                       38

**Stewart Lee.** The Homeland.                                        40

**Adam Buxton.** Brush.                                               42

**Simon Munnery.** If.                                                44

**Tim Key.** Selection.                                               46

**Russell Brand.** Feed Me.                                           48

**Tim Vine.** Limerick.                                               49

**Marek Larwood.** Bad Man.                                           50

**Owen O' Neill.** Drama in the Good Bookshop.                        52

**Simon Bird.** I love Vue.                                           53

**Anna Crilly.** The Fat Keeper's Sadness.                            54

**Arthur Smith.** If.                                                 55

**Ricky Grover.** Poems.                                              56

**Trevor Lock.** Haiku.                                      58

**Simon Munnery.** If London Could Speak.                    59

**Tim Key.** Trouble in the Woods.                           62

**Arthur Smith.** That's What he Would Have                  63
Wanted.

**Mark Watson.** Sad Friend.                                 64

**Simon Bird.** I Find the Current Government                66
Intolerable.

**Simon Day.** My Old Man.                                   68

**Boothby Graffoe.** A Thin Veneer of Eggshells              69
by Boothby Aged 9.

**Andy Zaltzman.** Albert Wole's Catapult of                 70
Truth.

**David Shrigley.** Who's Been Writing in my                 81
Diary?


**Contributors**                                             82

**& The People Who Put It Together**                         85

**Acknowledgements**                                         86

# FOREWORD

by Simon Munnery

## Comedy & Poetry

Comedy and poetry make strange bedfellows. Poetry gets up before dawn and downs an espresso to watch the sun rise, while comedy languishes in bed till noon, fiddling with itself and flicking channels. Poetry is prone to gazing at itself in the mirror in an ecstasy of despair. Comedy holds a mirror up to others then runs off giggling. Comedy likes big nights out and the roar of a crowd. Poetry prefers solitude and the roar of a waterfall. They both drink a lot. Perhaps that's why they end up in bed together. Poetry rarely swears; comedy does it all the time as if trying to wear out the words with overuse. Comedy shits its pants, Poetry doesn't wear any. It's a very messy house.

Tim Key

**368.**
'An ox!?'
I couldn't conceal my incredulity.
Why had she bought an ox?

Simon Munnery

**Oh Father**

Oh father I can feel
You standing at the end of my bed
Pulling the duvet and shouting
*Come on wakey wakey, rise and shine*
*What time do you call this, shake a leg*
Oh father put a sock in it
I've seen the clock and it's
No later than noon
I know only too well
This is not a hotel
You remind me every morning
And I remind you
I am considering
Checking out soon
And father you turn puce but what's the use
In arguing?

I always win after all
For you know and I know that although
The cold hard world is on your side
Mummy is on mine.

## Adam Buxton

### You're Getting Married

Marriage is a holy box
That doesn't need a key or locks.
You put in it your hopes and dreams.
It's also good for plans and schemes.
But loneliness you can't put in.
You have to keep that in a tin
With lust and hate and vice and sin.
And biscuits and pornography.

## Isy Suttie

### A Conversation with my Dad

Hi Dad, how are you?
*Your mother's at the church.*
What you been doing?
*Nothing. Trimmed that birch.*
Anything else?
*Killed some bees.*
Yes, the bees, it's hot
*Not like 1973.*
Dad, I need to tell you
*She's playing the piano.*
Something I've been wanting
*I just hit a bee, whammo!*
You to know for ages
*On its bum, smack!*
I miss you a bit.
*Sure, I'll tell yer mother when she's back.*


### My Dad's Watch

I said to my Dad,
*Your watch looks expensive*
He replied,
*It's an imitation of an imitation of a Rolex.*
When I graduated,
He punched me on the arm.
It was an imitation of an imitation of a hug.

Robert Newman

## The Invisible Republic

Beneath the streets
There is an alternative geography
The real map.

None of your old borders,
No names of kings or saints or generals
Are known here.

Railtracks swerve
At Tottenham North Curve Number 1.

In the sewers, London city limits are
The Northern Outfall and Southern Outfall.
Following the true map,
You catch the sidewinder Labrador Current
To the North Atlantic Gyre.

It's a workable world:
Digswell,
Dock Junction.
Fleet River Tunnel.

It's another world, one I'm less tired of.

There are many of us
who will declare ourselves for this,
Though we don't belong anywhere
And never thought we'd be doing any declaring.

These are signposts of the invisible republic,
The world which opens up to us
When we forget the rest.

# Wil Hodgson

## I'm A Man

I'm a man who at 17 wanted nothing more
Than to be a skinhead
And a man who stepped into the wrestling ring
For a brief but colourful period.

But also a man who's collected
Care Bears, My Little Pony's, Wuzzles, Popples,
Wild Puffalumps and Snugglebums
Pretty much all his life.

A man who despises war
For the senseless bloodshed it is
And views the Royal Family
As a ludicrous anachronism.

But also a man who's proud to say
He was a heavily decorated Sea Cadet
Who finds Sarah Ferguson incredibly sexual
(Chest flushes and all that).

A man who thinks that anyone
Who's ever bought, read,
Or even glanced at a lad's mag
Should be incinerated on a pyre of said publication.

But also a man who admires anyone
Who buys Reader's Wives
For their integrity and courage.

A man of many contradictions and contrasts
But a man all the same.

But according to cretins in polo shirts
Not a man at all.

# Arthur Smith

## Odd Sox

I've got 47 socks
Including  11 pairs
Lovers come and wear my socks
Move on and leave me theirs

Here's a red sock for example
Belonging once to Kim
She who now cooks lunch for Gary
This green sock belongs to him

Every sock can tell a story
They have ambitions of their own
When I'm out with 2 old favourites
Sometimes one does not come home

On my left foot there's a white sock
On my right foot there's a blue
Even though they smell somewhat
They make me think of you and you

People say odd sox is crazy
People say I'm queer
People say I've lost my marbles
Well I haven't- I've got them here

I've got 47 marbles
Including 11 pairs
Lovers come and roll my marbles
Move on and roll me theirs

## Robin Ince

**The inanimate are trying to destroy me**

Shouting at my own shoe laces
That unravel and trail as I hurry
For the late date that looms later
Their behaviour seems unruly
My knot was not at fault
It's them.

They want to trip me up, rip me up
Break my knees and watch me stumble
While a local boy on a bench
Laughs out loud
And places the cross on my grave marked
*Clumsy Twat. Slipped, tripped and mentally flipped,*
*Unable to rule his own shoes*
It is not me.

The inanimate are trying to destroy me.
This door, it sticks
It doesn't have to do but it does
And kicks
And screaming at it's pine won't budge it
It couldn't be my cack-handed carpentry
No this door holds some grudge
Won't budge
I'll win this one.
My angry foot creates a hole
Rubber sole trapped in an amateur cat flap
Of my own making
It's not my fault.

The inanimate are trying to destroy me
This laptop
Top notch collation of diodes
Is stuck on caps lock
Number lock
Refusing to obey me
My deadline is baying me

To somehow form a sentence
That this technology will understand

Numerals and capitals screech out
It taunts me with its whirring
A hi-tech snigger in my face
But I show it
With a swing that flings
The whole thing
Into a wall
It's not laughing now
And now neither am I
That's a fortune snapped, blank
Dead and empty

Why are the inanimate trying to destroy me?
I know the house is a mess
Of unhinged doors
Snapped technology
And ripped laces littering the floors
But don't blame me
If you'd only listen before you scold
I've told you
The objects all around are starting a revolution
A final solution
Against the flesh that tries to control them

The inanimate are trying to destroy me
And you'll be next

Oh okay, I'll fetch the vacuum cleaner
Suck up the detritus I have made
Henry Hoover's face looms
Voraciously sucks and tucks
Into my trail of carnage

Just remember
Keep your hem away from his revolving mouth
He might just be coming to destroy you

## Simon Bird

### Haiku

Ironically
This haiku's final word is
Monosyllabic.

# Tim Vine

**Film Poster**

There's an out of date film poster opposite my flat
on a 30 foot hoarding. Is someone still paying for that?
It was on at the Odeon about 3 years ago,
*'Unmissable'*
*'High Octane'*
*'Action Packed'*
*'You've Got To Go'*
I saw it when it was released I think.
Actually I can't remember much about it.
I expect they had fun making it. That's the main thing.

# Mark Watson

## The Changeover

i am a ballgirl at a major tennis tournament you
are the world number seventy-two my job
other than getting the ball back
is to attend to you at changeovers
for example i might fetch you water or a banana
or hold the parasol to shade you from the
heat of the mid-afternoon or look
discreetly away as you peel off a sweaty
shirt and replace it with a fresh one
my job other than getting the ball back
is emphatically not under any circumstances to
talk to you other than in the course of
carrying out your monosyllabic orders
i am not to disturb or harass you in any
way as you collect your thoughts for the fifth
set while on the other side of the chair your
opponent does the same thing
nevertheless it is very hard for me to watch you
hitting all these shots to his backhand as if
hoping to exploit a weakness because it has
become clear over the past four sets that he
not only possesses a very good backhand but
is able to anticipate your constant cross-court
shots and put himself in a great position to
bang them back down the line as i say you
are the world number seventy-two and i
am probably not even the best ballgirl here
sara is more elegant certainly and rachael
got to shake hands with the queen last year
but i just think you should be looking to
play on his lack of pace which will be
more and more evident as fatigue kicks in
especially as this sun continues to burn
down i think you should be coming forward
much more and hitting drop shots and mixing
it up a bit i must emphasise once again you are
the expert here you are the one who plays
22

tennis for a living i am still at
art college and i don't ever expect to be seen
by as many people at one time as there are
here watching you so feel free to play it your
way of course i just think at the risk of repeating
myself you have to capitalise on his
tired legs well anyway the umpire is
about to call time so instead of giving you all this
tactical advice i will keep silent and refill
the water bottle and hand it to you and you
will acknowledge it without looking at me
and i will see you when you are next down
this end i guess in a few games' time

## Phil Nichol

### Kill Yourself

actions

speak louder

than words

except when

words

can't describe

the action

and the action

becomes

looking for words

impressed

no?

then kill yourself.

# Steve Hall

## a poem i sent a girl when i was seventeen and scary

o Jessamy, o Jessamy
i know that you want less o'me
but if you just say yes to me
we'll make the perfect recipe
our hearts will open sesame
my love's like a colostomy bag
you slag
fancy a shag?

## Paul Foot

### Somme Mothers Do 'Ave 'Em

How we suffer, with our modern-age woes:
Allergic to wheat, milk and things like those.

In the trenches, they had no dinner choice
Would a mother have heard her husband's voice:

'Ooh Betty, dreadful news- our son is dead
He starved; because, you see, he ate no bread.'

Then, men were brave; but now- without a Kraut
They need something else to be brave about.

Instead of monuments to war deceased
Let's build them for those who avoided yeast.

*Rose Ann Hurfield fought gluten for years*
*And lactose was another of her fears.*

*Danny Drips was intolerant to fish*
*After plaice and chips, he died in anguish.*

Andrew Maxwell

**Hello Heckler**

Make ya feel stupid
Then I'll do it again
Make ya feel crowded
Like a battery hen

Hold out the little hand of hope
You got an answer, just enough rope

Now you're feelin dizzy
In this mess of your makin'
I'm a verbal cannibal
And I can smell bacon...

# Harry Hill

## The Pistachio

He stalks the earth
Like a hermit crab
Ne'er leaving his shell
To he, we are like
Flounder or dab
Condemning his flesh to hell!
Out! Out!
Green Nutty lump!
And let me gorge on thy flesh
With a drink.

## The Monkey Nut

Phwoar look at her!
With her hour glass figure
Struttin' like a prozzie
Cos her baby's in town.
She's a monkey nut and don't she know it!
See how the bar tender whistlers
*Give us a peek at your twin milky whites!*
Cries he.
Caressing her with his thumb
Standing by the bin
To make it easier
To put her skin in
it.

### The Walnut

Like a rubber ball
You come bouncing back to me!
Bouncy Bouncy!
Bouncy Bouncy!
Bouncy Bouncy!
Bouncy Crack!
Ah ha!
Eugh!
Yuk!
Bitter.

Tony Law

**The Sausage Inquisition**

Cartridge Davison and Alberta Law
took on the Spanish Inquisition.
*Did it by undermining then's time.*
Looked back and mocked them
from the relative safety of now and where.

'Could Cesc Fabregas have been an inquisitivor?'
Asked Alberta Law the sausage dog.
'That ain't no word'
Said Cartridge Davison who had no grasp of grammar or
punctuation. And too was a wiener dog.
'My ass is itchy.... there, I have gnawed on it with my teeth
and it is better now.'
'Now, it seems to me dear girl Alberta,
That human beings have evolved  themselves into a bind.
They are smart, but not so smart.
They fear death and make up fantasy and more fear.
They blow themselves and others up.
They blow. This I like.
They cant keep things in their head.
On the whole I like them, for they make me laugh.
Sometimes they are cocks though.'

'I thinks so too' Alberta Law barked.
'The Cock bit'

'You said thinks' Cartridge Davison added added.
'They hate that in Spain of the past, but they no can do
nuttin about it, and you just added added.'

'Ha were done now'
'Was that a poem?'
'It is not for us to decide what is a poem, for us it is
enough to mock the Spanish Inquisition,
and all of the selfish, vain, fantasist, misogynist,
*'Victim' 'Poor Me'* human mental nutbars.'

'And Wahhabists?'
'Sure, why not?'
'Poor point'
'Fag'
'What?'
'Smokes'
'Oh.'

# Arthur Smith

## And Drunk

Your eyes are red
Your teeth are yellow
You're really not
An appealing fellow
You're going bald
You've grown a belly
It's not enough
To be on telly.

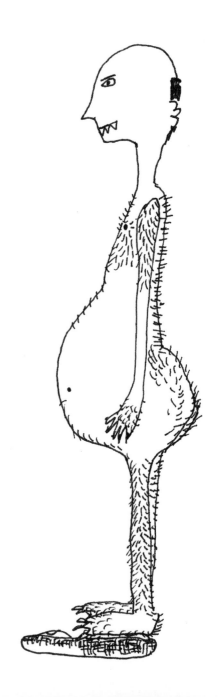

# Josie Long

## The first time my mum met my boyfriend

We went to a Turkish restaurant
and I didn't have enough money to pay so she treated us.
I wanted her to be stiff and semi-formal
and for the whole thing to be like it was in the 1950's.
I started conversations about how he was a teacher
but she had to bring up the men she was meeting
from an advert she put in the 'news shopper'
and I ate tsatsiki and looked down at the table
while she said
*I mean, one didn't have any testicles*
*and the other had false teeth!*
*What am I supposed to do?*
*Choose between testicles and teeth?*
*What would you choose Matthew?*
and I spat out a bit of kofte.
He tried to respond
but it wasn't what my mum wanted to hear.
And she said to me
*What do you think I should do dear?*
and I didn't know where I could start.
So I said

'The food is really good isn't it,
Have you had one of these aubergines?'

# Simon Day

## The Bold Peanut

Last night at 8.15 one of my peanuts made a break for it
dry roasted he was or should have been
perhaps somehow he had dodged the process
did he think I was some kind of fool?
*I watched him scrambling towards the door!*
He was creating his own momentum.
*Outstanding, a peanut!*
I checked the remaining nuts;
quiet, still, salty well behaved.

No mutiny.

Was he attempting to leave snackworld?
Had he foreseen a better life in a dream?
He was taking the piss as far as I was concerned.
Eventually his pathetic limping roll
caused something to snap in my brain
I picked him up, halved him,
there was no device inside, no jumping thing
I put both halves down on the table
and went out for beers.

I am older now and I wonder
if that night meant something?
I hope he's still out there doing the do!
I wonder if the the two halves got back together?
Maybe one half is a millionaire and the other a bum.
I am getting married soon and I worry
he will do something to ruin our day.

## Simon Munnery

**Were I to be asked again**

Were I to be asked again
And I consider it unlikely
Mid conversation in a social situation
Who might I be and what exactly it was
I did for a living
I would reply: *I am Artist*
If they were then to correct
You mean an artist surely
I would exclaim:
*What! There are others? We must meet*
Turn on my feet and skip skip skip away
And I would continue skipping
Until I got on their nerves.

If on the other hand they were to ask
What sort of art it was that I made
I would explain:
*My art! Consist! Of Repeating Phrase–*
*I am Artist! In Situation: This!*

If they then asked me
How I made money doing it
I would mug them.
For more than an artist
I am a kind of teacher.

Boothby Graffoe

**The little known Freudian slip of Martin
Luther King.**

I have a dream. *People!* I have a dream!
I see a white man, I see a black woman
I see them being wed
I see them lying in slumber
In the privacy of their nuptial bed.
I see them lying together, in beautiful love
Naked! Yet blending, like coffee and cream.
I hear gasps and sighs
I see breasts and thighs. *Good Lord!*

Oh my mistake...
Wrong dream.

# Dan Antopolski

## These Are Three Fridge Magnet Poems I Done

*The first was backstage at Swansea University on a filing cabinet, where I piously sought to reclaim some tenderness from an 'erotic' vocabulary set which some twenty year olds - now my tribal enemies - had arranged with a buttheaded lack of intervention. It is about a loss of innocence.*

Would there burn a passion
an agony of joy
let love shudder in the neverwoman boy
hard then languid
he murmurs every language
come perfectly to his full say so

*Now this is a passive-aggressive poem written on my uncle's fridge one christmas*

the summer's lazy light cooks me weakly through
essential as blood
then winter waxes with the smell of hot chocolate
language or tv
roads under flood
how are you two
produce a black friend
as a playful power gift I club your puppy to death
beneath the moon and an eternity of frantic void
we recall his hairy rust and always licking tongue
diamond is gone

*While this last deals with the beginnings of life itself*

swim to the egg
incubate
head through the rose petals
cool

*It may be short but it has already been reviewed ["Romanticised" - F.Beard]*

*That is all*

Alex Horne

**Why Some Birds Look Pissed Off**

Bee-eaters are glamourous birds,
Bright orange and yellow and blue.
They fly in formation and sing like a choir,
And they're pretty good whistlers too.
It's the fact that they've been named
'Bee-eaters'
That has put them in quite a bad mood–
It's certainly odd to eat insects that sting,
But why only highlight
Their odd taste in food?

A warbler must also feel slightly ripped off,
By their clearly pejorative name.
While the thrasher, the babbler,
The godwit, and snipe,
I'm pretty sure all feel the same.
Chickens insist that they can be quite brave,
And pigeons just hate the name 'pigeon'.
But at least they're the most
Well-known bird of that sound
Because nobody's heard of the wigeon

It's easy to taunt a canada goose:
Just say that you thought it American.
While reciting the rhyme
Will annoy the famed bird
Whose beak can hold more than its belly can.
And we all mock those poor innuendoful birds
Like the tits and the cocks and the peckers,
The boobies, the shags, the swallows, the thrush,
And the rare yellow-bellied sapsuckers.

The grouse says he wishes he wasn't so famous,
Bald eagles are plausibly flustered.
The twite says he sounds
Like you're slagging him off,

But not nearly as much as the bustard.
*We all have bad hair days* cries the old tufted duck,
*I normally sport a side-parting*
And that's just plain lazy,
Says the swallow's best mate,
*You can't call an animal 'martin'*

But though these birds are justifiably miffed
By names that sound bollo or highlight odd features,
They're still better off than another winged being–
The worst of the worst of the badly-named creatures.
And it's no surprise these things spend all their lives
Making mind-numbing noises,
Polluting the skies,
And generally seeking to reek some revenge
On the people who thought that their name
Should be 'flies'.

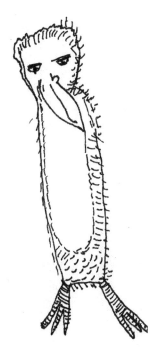
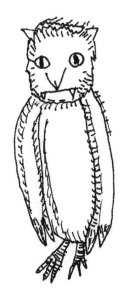

Stewart Lee

## The Homeland

Americans gather in County Clare
At breakfast time in cooing pairs
And tell us of this land of theirs.

They have used their two weeks holiday
To experience their epiphany
Of racial identity.

Australians in Europe pass by
The scenes of their grandparents' crimes
Looking for cheap booze and good times.

But Americans in Ireland seem
Cowed by the hills and streams
Treading softly on their dreams.

In the shadow of Carrowkee
An American at the wheel
Explains how dismayed he feels

That the grave of his ancestor
Hides up high in hillside heather
Inaccessible to the visitor.

In the field at Carrowmore
The Americans are bored
By the subterranean horde

Because there's nothing to be seen
But depressions in the green
Where something might have been.

But at the Shelagh Na Gig in Sligo
There's a session on the go
Fiddle and bodhran.

An American crowds my space
His fat arse is in my face
He tries to understand

But rebel songs remain unsung
Jigs and reels go on too long
And he shuffles to the door

Leaving behind his daughter
At the feet of Brian McDonagh
Cross legged on the floor.

This trip meant nothing to her
Her parents stole her summer
And she hates her little brother
But at the feet of Brian McDonagh
Playing his mandola
Something stirs inside her
And she's happy for a while.

## Adam Buxton

### Brush

It takes so long to wash black paint out
From a great big brush
But it's important to be thorough
It's not a job to rush.

You don't want any black blobs
To nestle at the bristle root
Or one day later in your life
When you paint a shelf,
Or maybe a door,
And you're not using black no more
The blobs will come back out again
And make you want to shoot yourself
Because your shelf
Is smeared with grey.

Then you will regret the day
You put that fucking brush away.

## Simon Munnery

### If

IF
You know what it's like
To look back on your life
And think my God I was an idiot then
And in the same breath
To suffer the glimpse:
You're and idiot now and shall be till the end
THEN
Come away from that mirror my friend
Cease your melancholy reflection
You're a prisoner of habit
Trapped like a rabbit
In the headlights
Of its own demise
You might be sailing across an ocean
You might be sailing across a lake
But how can you steer, staring at your wake?
Better calm down lift up thine eyes 'cause
It don't matter none
And if you need a blinding light
If you need a blinding light
If you need a blinding light
Try the sun
You can look back at how far you've come
You can never return to your mum
You can only proceed by rule of thumb
So lift up thine eyes it don't matter none
All your opinion all your frustration
You know we leave shadows two centuries long
And it's not the singer that redeems the song
But the listening ear oh my darling there's an
End to fear and it won't be long so come on

And if you need a blinding light
If you need a blinding light
And one day you just might
Try the son
And remember:
In Russia
Nostalgia is regarded as an Illness
So they say
Or rather, it used to be
In the good old days.

# Tim Key

## Selection

**116.**
One ant
Wrote on his C.V.
That he'd carried a piano.
He implied
He'd carried it alone.

**139.**
I tried bribing the P.C.
She called me cute and cuffed me.
My jeans were lank with blood.

**263.**
Webbsy - my vole - has been stolen.
My only hope is that he's been stolen by someone who's
owned a vole with Webbsy's unique
catalogue of problems before.

**306.**
Dillip, Bill, Ollie Wade, Stuart Gunn, Al Gunn
and P.L.R. Hancock
CLUBBED TOGETHER
And bought Toby Webber - the student councillor - a
mirror with a plaque under it which had the words
'mickey-taking arsehole' engraved on it.

**277.**
Harold said 'water water everywhere
but not a drop to drink'.
But in totally the wrong context.
And -rightly- he was shot in the head.

**285.**
Craig Hut shaved his hair off on the Monday
And did his first baldy headbutt on the Friday
(In the town centre).

**280.**
Robbie
Broke his own heart
When he told his own bathroom mirror
'You're impossible to love, Robbie Matthews'.

**286.**
'You shouldn't use such a big spoon!' I heard
my wife giggle through the partition.
I retreated to the golfing range and struck some drives.
Clearly Luther or someone was now *feeding my wife* in
the afternoons.

**298.**
BABY-FACED ASSASSIN
Baby faced assassin.
And was shot by assassin.

**305.**
A fit student
Dressed in a flimsy green top
Waltzed around the Union
Singing up-to-date pop songs
And making her insubstantial black skirts jump up.
Craig -a suicidal fourth year-
sipped his Guinness and watched.

**312.**
A beautiful Japanese girl -slim hips-
Smiles a thin smile when taking the money
From the businessmen she fucks.
(She is a professional whore).

**325.**
The Blind Politician -
'BLUNKETT'
Scratched his balls and told a hundred lies.
Then he cuddled his dog and ordered his manservant to
make him a curry as hot as his hat.

Russell Brand

**Feed Me**

'All them girls…'
(pause)
'You must be like a kid in a sweet shop,'
He said.
I pondered.
If you were a kid in a sweet shop,
The first half hour would be nice.
*Mmmmmm, sweets* you'd think, *Delicious!*
You'd cram caramel into your lusty gut
Scoff toffees and gobble choc drops
Yielding to the spirit of Bacchus.
You'd gorge on sherbert mountains
And guzzle fizzy pop lagoons.

But in the moons glare when
The sweet shop bristled
With hollow lonely clicks
You'd squirm.

Dull looming jars. Bereft of treats.
Floor strewn with curly whirly corpses,
Like a Columbine on Wonka's factory floor,
Slaughtered oompa loompas twitching by the counter.
Then the demons would come.
You'd paw the indifferent glass, cold like Spandau walls
'What wouldn't I give for a sprout'
you'd mutter as you died of diabetes.
He reflected; 'Still, all them girls…'

# Tim Vine

## Limerick

There was an old man from Limerick,
Who was completely unaware of the short and often
Humorous poems that shared the
Same name as his home town.

# Marek Larwood

**Bad Man**

A man walked past me. As he went he whispered that he was lonely. So I followed him, curious as to whether he had some sweets. Later it became clear that he had no sweets whatsoever, and was a bad man. Watch out for people who match his description. He had hair, shoes, and was wearing a coat.

*

I opened my curtains again this morning, and the bad man was there. He wanted to come in as he was cold and had forgotten his clothes. I said *'This better not be a lie bad man'*. Soon after I found out it was a lie.

*

Today when I opened the curtains the bad man wasn't there. Part of me felt lonely. Then because I felt lonely, I felt dirty. *'He is a bad man, he is a bad man!'* I told myself by shouting at the top of my voice. I did not feel better, so I went into the garden and threw some stones at the next-door neighbour's cat who is an arsehole.

*

I opened the curtains this morning, I saw the bad man again. But he was across the road outside Peter Smithson's window. Peter Smithson always gets everything he wants, the best bicycles, the best trainers, the best packed lunches. He sits at the back of the bus like he is some big cheese, talking really loudly like a real life microphone might. I hope Peter Smithson steps in some dog's mess.

*

Peter Smithson has been missing for three days now. I went round to Peter Smithson's house, to see if I could have his bike as he was missing. His Mum said no, and that he was on holiday with his Dad.

*

Peter Smithson's parents are dicks, just like him.

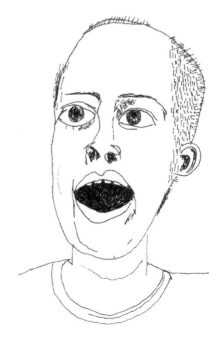

Owen O'Neill

**Drama in the good bookshop**

Oh my God!

There it was, shamelessly white and long, perched
in her brown tipped fingers, smouldering.

She sucked upon it, collapsing her face. Then
talked out the smoke. Replying to the young
assistant, who looked younger.

'Well!' she shrieked, looking for a sign
'where does
it say you must not smoke?' I too searched
desperately for a sign.

'There is none,' said the young assistant in a
strong bookish voice free from wheeze. 'Well then,'
she squawked. 'What do you expect?' And was gone
leaving the puff of smoke, wafting, unable to
defend itself.

'What a stupid old cunt' said the young assistant
spoiling the moment.

Simon Bird

**I Love Vue**

We went to the cinema together,

well, with a group of friends.

I got Pick n' Mix

and offered you some.

You took a fried egg.

It was the best movie

since Con Air.

# Anna Crilly

## The Fat Keeper's Sadness

You cannot watch Neil Morrissey
work his canny magic
You cannot stroke the crocodile
down at County Fagic (Zoo)
You'll never enjoy reclining
on a deck chair in the sun
And don't wish for a lover
you'll never meet 'the one'

You'll never own an empire
You'll never catch a fish
You miss out on a lot of things
when you're a butter dish.

## Arthur Smith

### If

If you can roll along at a decent pace
And you find that your rear
Contains lots of space
If you have windows at the front
Yet none at the side
And offer a smooth unflashy ride
If you have a red and white flag
On your bonnet
And can never imagine doing a ton
Then yours is the road and everything on it
And, which is more, you'll be a van, my son.

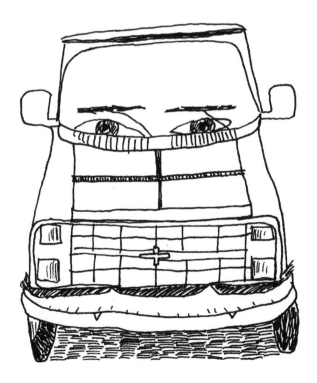

# Ricky Grover

## First Poem

I cunt spell,
and I find it hard to make things rhyme,
So whose idea was it to do a poem,
becoz it sertainly wasn't mine?

People say I never see the obvious,
perhaps they think I'm thick,
But I like to weigh up the more important things in life,
Like what makes a suicide bomber tick?
Sweet!

# Ricky Grover

## Second Poem

When I was a young chavvy
growing up in the East End,
We didn't 'ave a shilling,
So we chored what we could
to try and nick a living,
Some of my old muckers got trapped
in the circle of villainy,
But all they've ever done is fight back
at this corrupt society,
Yes they've robbed banks.
But banks rob people all the time,
So I find the whole scenario satisfyingly sublime
I don't even know what sublime means
but it nearly made a ryme.

I'll wrap this up by asking you a question,
Then I'll end on a suggestion,
How can a paedafile only get six months
community service for hurting a little child,
And a man who robs a bank gets a twenty stretch?
The answer to this question is really plain to see,
The judge has more in common with the nonce than
he has with thieves like me.
God Bless.

Trevor Lock

**Haiku**

A hot summer night,
I took off my tight trousers
And then she took off.

## Simon Munnery

### If London Could Speak

Where am I from?
I'm from Ypres and the Somme
Passchendaele and Verdun
Saigon, Lebanon,
Srebrenica - on and on

Don't ask me where I'm blinking from:
I am London
Come to kill you
Come to bill you
Come to take your eyes

I am the stones, the bones, the traffic cones
The aches and pains,
The pissed-up shagged-out manky brains
I am what remains
In the morning sun
When you've had your fun

I am London
And I say Come to me! Come to me!
Wherever you are
Come to me!
Bring your car
And you'll come

For two weeks that'll turn into ten years
'Till your skin's falling off and you think
*Oh I'd better get out of London*
*Now me skin's falling off*
Now it's too bloody late

But where you going to go?
Out to the countryside to have kids
Settle down in the countryside with your kids

Thinking
*Oh I'm out in the countryside with my kids*
*I got away from London*
*I got away from London*

But no you ain't: You got kids
And where are they coming?
Back to London that's where

You've got to run
Just to stand still
Don't even think
About being ill

You can have a quickie take a sickie
Do what you got to do
But don't take the micky
Beggars can't be choosers
You can't be picky
Get it? Got it? Good
Off you go now son
Off to those fields to breed
Or lie in that gutter and bleed

I am London
Infinite city
Mighty pretty
And mighty ugly too
'Cause an infinite city is an infinite city
That means: it's bigger than you:
I'm going to crush your nuts

Rome; The Eternal City
That's what they say in Rome
Bit presumptuous of them really
Time ain't quite finished yet
But if Rome can be the eternal city
Then London can be the infinite city

It takes two and a half hours
To drive across London
In an hour and a quarter you can fly to Rome
That makes Rome a suburb.

# Tim Key

## Trouble In The Woods

*Because you're a smartarse*
*and you always have been!*
Winnie-The-Pooh aimed another blow
to owl's beak (or what was left of it)
Piglet loyally continued to ransack the house.
*Shit on his encyclopedias, too!*
Pooh ordered his lover.

Appendix-
Injuries sustained by owl: poked out eye; damaged beak; cut off
feet; charred feathers.

# Arthur Smith

## That's What He Would Have Wanted

Joint before I left
Cigarettes in the heat-free Merc
Following the hearse
For him it must have got worse

Crowding in the confused church
Longing for a fag
And one less verse
For him it must have got worse

The day he got buried
Was brittle, painful, cold
Shivering girls
In long black dresses
Big boots and earring in the nose
This is not a funeral
For someone old

The music falters by the grave
Funny, sad
For him it must have got too bad

# Mark Watson

## sad friend

i thought we were meeting for tea just
the two of us but then shortly beforehand
you called and said is it all right if i
bring my friend
she's sad at the moment
she's going through some weird stuff at the moment
she's just a bit down at the moment
of course i said of course i mean
what kind of a heartless bastard
would snub someone who is having
such a difficult few moments
all the same it did mean that while
i was looking forward to talking in quite
a lot of detail about your hatred of
your brother's girlfriend
and your continued reluctance to be treated
like an idiot by your immediate so-called superior
in the office
we instead discussed in the most superficial manner
topics which would include all three of us
which inevitably was a rather shorter shallower list
and all the while your sad friend sat there
looking down at the table
mulling over the problems she has at the moment
smiling a watery smile when prodded into
conversation
ordering tea in a near inaudible voice
and thinking throughout
i shouldn't be here
i am just getting in the way
i am not adding anything to this
everyone is going to get tired of having me here
which is the sort of thing liable to become
a self-fulfilling prophecy

## Simon Bird

### I find the current government intolerable

FUCK
The war in IRAQ.

TONY, you don't fool us anymore,
You've befooled us before
With your preschool of misrule,
Your smile of bile, your tool of cool,
It makes us drool a black pool
CONFERENCE.

TONY, or should I say SATAN,
You slither like a spiteful snake in Eden,
Shedding your outer cast so as to reveal a new cast
which you will probably shed again next year in
much the same manner.
You moult truth
And now you LIE.

In the grass.

Basking.

MONEY, MONEY, MONEY – that's your life.
'Honey I'm-'
It's your bubble bubble trouble and strife.
She's what makes your heart flutter.
You coalesce and mutter
DARK ART. As ravens circle
You MAKE HELL.
It's pretty please and Cherie's on top – a BAKEWELL
Tart.

Oh my apologies.
Do I cut too deep?
Do I rhyme too hard?
Do I make you weep?
I'M DYING for a cup of cha.


Pass me Heat magazine, ah,
Look at the size of Trevor McDonald's thumb.
A-list, B-list, I can't SEE through the MIST
Of Blair's **GREAT FAT FAILURE.**

Simon Day

**My Old Man**

My old man's a dustman,
And he wears a dustman's hat,
He wears cor-blimey trousers,
And he lives in a council flat.

He's finished work by one o' clock,
And spends the rest of the day wanking,
And watching the races.

Boothby Graffoe

## A Thin Veneer of Eggshells by Boothby aged 9

I am a twat
I am aware of that
I have a hat,
with 'twat' written on it.
An honesty bonnet
And when people say
You're a twat
I say, I know
Look at my hat,
You twat.

# Andy Zaltzman

## Albert Wole's Catapult of Truth

The village fete of '82 and the name of Albert Wole
Are bound together in eternity
By the man's intrepid soul.
That day, he declared an intention
To defy convention
And become the first man in history to reach the moon
By catapult.
'The guy's a loon'
The consensus gloated.
'He'll spoil the festivities
With his aerial proclivities'
Cackled the villagers, bloated
As they were on traditional village fete activities,
Such as: looking at tables full of things,
Guessing the number of things in other things,
And throwing things at other things.
Things can be educational as well as fun. Point proved.
Britain loves things.

At 3pm, Albert moved.
He emerged from his shed,
Wherein his psychological preparation
For hyperstratospheric elevation
Involved flinging six-inch porcelain dolls of himself
At a moon-shaped object on a wonky shelf.
I think it was a plate.
Yes, it was a plate.
He hadn't hit one yet, thus negating his greatest fear:
Peaking too soon,
And risking missing the real moon.

Cocooned in his own private destiny,
Albert prepared for launch.
The tension grew like a fox.
Flaunting an imposing paunch,
The local mayor came forward from the crowd.
Though no-one recognised him, he seemed enthusiastic,

So was allowed
To don what he claimed were ceremonial socks,
And slit the throat
Of the official goat,
Whose collapsing corpse would release
The catch on the cage door of the geese
Who had been trained to flock
Onto a set of scales, which unbalanced
Would tip a small rock
Onto the head of the local MP,
Who would be reminded to remind Albert Wole that he
Should pull the lever to set the catapult in motion.

A sudden commotion–
A cheer rose to the skies,
But to Albert's surprise,
The din was not for him,
But for Mrs Pimm,
Headmistress of the village school,
Who broke her own unbending rule
By shouting aloud,
Dropping her trousers and mooning the crowd.
The village caterwauled their approval as one.
But only years later did Pimm receive full credit
For her brilliant visual pun.

Following a semi-amusing dummy sacrifice,
One slash of the mayoral knife was enough to suffice.
And as the earth teemed
With his blood, the dying goat seemed
To mouth the words: 'Why? Why?
When will the killing end?'
Seemed to, but didn't. He was a goat. Let's not pretend
Otherwise. What he actually mouthed was: 'I am a goat,
And I am dying of a very serious injury to the throat.'

Twang.

Albert flew, flew up and away, through the air,
Over the bouncy castle, where
The local terrorists hid in a group,
Over the swings, where a satirical mime troupe
Was impersonating public opinion, over a foal...
But, just as it seemed that he might well be able
To attain the moon and achieve his goal,
Albert crashed, screaming, into an overhead power cable.

Now, in itself, this would not necessarily have been
Fatal for Albert. For this he'd foreseen,
And was wearing a special moon-suit made of wood,
Which didn't conduct electricity, and therefore could
Be worn with confidence and impunity,
Except around fires.
Besides which there was no power in the wires
Because no-one in the village had plugs.

The crowd gasped, momentarily forgetting the drugs
Scandal that had rocked the tombola
When old Mrs Zola
Tested positive for a banned anabolic steroid.
The bottle of Scotch she'd won was declared void,
And she was hounded away,
But to this day,
The stain, and the pain, remain.

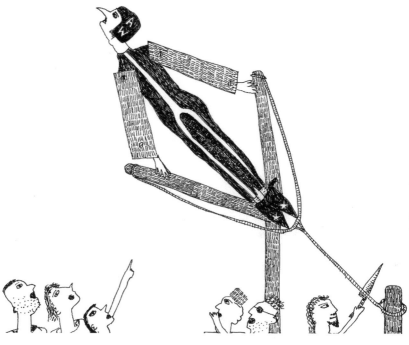

But then, just as it seemed that Albert might survive,
The elastic effect of the cables came alive,
And flang him back across the village at some speed.
(Some speed, but not all speed;
There was still a bit of speed
Left over for other things to continue moving).

The lunar journey was proving
Even tougher than Albert had anticipated.
Back he flew over the fete, over the bookmaker's tent,
Where an elated
Vicar was collecting his winnings from a bet
On exactly how much debt
His wife was in after her failed attempt to make it big
By breeding the world's first kosher pig.
He flew over the village store

Which didn't sell groceries any more,
And had been struggling ever since it began to specialise
In rotating stages instead.  All eyes
Followed Albert's struggling parabola across the skies.
'Could he still make the moon?' asked the people,
Until he landed stomach - first on the point
Of the church steeple.

Now, in itself, this would not necessarily
Have been fatal for Albert.  For the previous year,
The council had summarily
Had the steeple blunted,
After misinterpreting a new European directive.
The culprit, Councillor Pook, a witless man,
Was mercilessly hunted,
And bombarded with torrents of invective
Because his error had left the entire village in
Contravention
Not only of the new legislation, but also
Of the old convention
It was supposed to have replaced.
Oh, bureaucracy.

But then, just as it began to seem
That Albert might survive, the church was blown up
By a demolition team.
In the local recent election, the village had voted
Atheist, much to the disappointment of God,
Who was later quoted
As admitting that he had lost touch
With the crucial floating voters, who wield so much
Power these days.  He'd been complacent, God admitted,
And over the last two thousand years or so, had acquitted
Himself very poorly, considering the range
Of powers at his disposal. It really was time for a change.

Albert was in trouble.
He tumbled groundwards amidst the holy rubble,
His bubble
Of optimism burst,
And now, like a vegetarian German, he feared the worst.

But, incredibly, none of the cascade of masonry fell
On him – it was impossible to tell
Whether this was by divine providence,
Secular providence,
Or just plain luck.
Most of it, to universal delight, instead struck
The village library. No-one likes a smart arse.

Embarrassed by the burgeoning farce,
Albert, the failed lunar aviator
Covered his face in shame,
And therefore would not have seen
The church bell, which had been
Designed and built by a cartoon animator,
Realise it was no longer supported,
Look downwards to the ground in terror,
Metal face contorted
In comic grimace, then hang
Suspended in air for a humorously elongated moment,
Then plummet
From its former summit
Directly onto Albert with a hilarious clang.

Now, in itself, this would not necessarily have been
Fatal for Albert. For, as we have seen,
He was a tough man, and though the cartoon bell was
Comedically great,
It lacked any actual physical weight.

But then, as Albert rose from the wreck of the church,
He tripped on a stray lectern, and, with a lurch,
Stumbled and trod on an unexploded canister
Of poison gas –
A long - forgotten relic from a long-forgotten mass,
Which got out of hand when a single errant snore
During a touchy sermon provoked an all-out war.
Britain and Portugal fought for five long years
In the mid-seventies, but the war was never publicised,

Because the media had realised
That it was more fun to write about lost dogs than the
War's blood and tears.

Now, in itself, this would not necessarily
Have been fatal for Albert, because for years, he had
Ordinarily
Slept in a tiny cubby hole underground,
And thus had found
That he could learn to get by without oxygen–
The most arrogant of gases.
'Breathe me or you'll die.'
It hates the freedoms of the masses.

But just as it seemed that he'd survive intact,
At that very moment his thirty-year pact
With the devil expired,
And the servants of Satan, as the contract required,
Emerged from pub, and escorted Albert off to be hurled
Into his eternal underworld.

And Albert felt a pang of regret,
And began to fret
That he'd wasted his agreed 30 years of diabolic force
Being phenomenal at crosswords,
Rather than shaping the course
Of history to his own well-meaning masterplan.
'Ah well'
He thought, as he entered Hell.
Hindsight,
Schmindsight.

Now, in itself, this would not necessarily have been
Fatal for Albert, for Satan, though unquestionably mean,
Is a stickler for paperwork, and Albert's entry form
Had not been signed and dated, as was the norm.
So, after an angry pause,
The Devil released him on a hastily drafted
Three-week extension clause.

Albert crawled out of the depths, into the light,
But to the crowd who had once cheered him in flight,
He had failed,
So homewards they trailed.

They wanted a winner,
Not a resurfacing sinner.
At least, it seemed, he had survived his heroic,
Abortive mission.
But at that very moment, Albert died
Of a hereditary heart condition.

Again, in itself, this would not necessarily have been
Fatal for Albert, for whilst at the undertakers awaiting his
Final earthly preen,
He remembered that there was in fact no history
Of cardiac disease in his family. The mystery
Of his apparent death was easy to explain:
He had recently watched a TV documentary about fatal
Aortic strain,
And, though not easily stressed,
He was easily impressed.

On realising his error,
He sat up in terror,
Banged his head on his coffin lid,
And, knocked out cold, slid,
Unconscious, into a deep,
And hugely regrettable, sleep.

Albert died, a short hearse journey and a blessing later,
Of 100 per cent burns.

Whether Albert then went to meet his creator,
Or whether his remains simply remained
In his two self-made urns
No-one may know.

But his catapult failure,
Although (obviously) a personal blow,
As it unfurled
Taught invaluable lessons to the watching world

Namely: that ignorance of our own past
Can bring ultimate devastation;
That Devils are least dangerous when held fast
In the grip of bureaucratic legislation;
That not all wars receive the coverage they deserve;
That God and democracy do not mix;
That Britain's continuing ignorance about
Europe will serve
Only to exacerbate our bureaucratic fix;

And that catapults,
Although a flawed method of transport,
Can reveal the truth about everything.

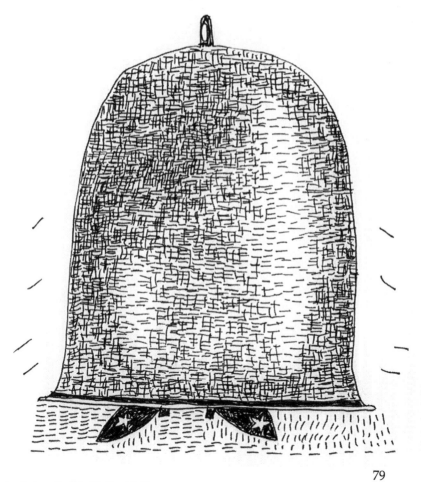

David Shrigley

**Writing In My Diary**

Who's been writing in my diary?

Writing about things I haven't done

And thoughts I haven't had

Saying I love people

Who I don't love

And that I hate people

Who I don't hate

And how were they

Able to copy my handwriting

So accurately?

# Contributors (in no order whatsoever)

### Alex Horne
Alex Horne is an award-winning (& losing) stand up comedian whose hobbies include Latin, puns, football &, most recently, bird watching. He has met and shaken paddles with the current Pope.

### Trevor Lock
Trevor Lock was created by Swiss scientists in a petri dish in 1979. After a catalogue of frankly unbelievable incidents he ended up living in a pink jumper in smug London & doing comedy.

### Phil Nichol
Born in Glasgow, raised in Toronto & lives in London. Phil would love to follow in the footsteps of legendary rock band Europe & have a number one hit in Japan.

### Boothby Graffoe
Sniff sniff.

### Marek Larwood
Marek Larwood is a comedian, he is one third of sketch group *We are Klang*, & he thinks cats are vermin who should be killed.

### Arthur Smith
Arthur Smith was the chairman of the University of East Anglia & was quoted by bookies at 250-1 to become poet laureate. He is the mayor of Balham (self appointed).

### Steve Hall
Steven Hall was born in Borehamwood in 1976. He now lives in London & does comedy. He supports Southampton FC & the death penalty.

### Stewart Lee
Stewart is a stand up comic, writer, music critic, DJ & director. He returns to the Fringe for the 18th time in 2006 to direct *Talk Radio* at the Udderbelly.

### Tim Vine
Tim Vine is a stand up comic. He specialises in quick fire puns. He holds the world record for most jokes told in an hour - 499.

### Anna Crilly
Stand up comedian & one half of sketch show *Penny Spubb* Anna can also be seen on the telly in Jack Dee's sitcom *Lead Balloon, Extras,* & Armando Iannucci's *Time Trumpet.*

### Tim Key
Tim writes poems for adults & children alike & recites them live in a lager-stained suit to an accompaniment of Soviet lounge music. He also writes bittersweet dramas for Radio 4 & has recently made a naturist silent movie.

## Simon Bird

Simon Bird is a comic actor, writer, & stand-up. He was a member of the Cambridge Footlights and took part in their 2006 Edinburgh show *Niceties*.

## Wil Hodgson

More of a raconteur/storyteller than an actual stand up, Wil Hodgson won the Perrier Best Newcomer Award in 2004. He likes Oi! music, Care Bears, & books of bare ladies.

## Isy Suttie

Isy's well known on the national circuit for her songs, weird stories, & characters. She appeared in the *Comedy Zone Edinburgh 2005*, and *Take-a-Break Tales 2006*. Chortle Award nominee 2005, she's also a qualified wine advisor.

## Harry Hill

Harry Hill is Britain's foremost foraging comedian, surviving almost entirely on nuts and berries which he is able to turn directly into adrenaline for purposes of excitement

## Simon Day

Simon Day is a Fool. Sometimes for cash. He lives in the space between hey-hum and hey-ho.

## Ricky Grover

Born & bred in London's East End & illiterate until the age of thirty, Ricky is an ex-boxer and hairdresser. Award winning actor, writer, comedian, & poet?

## Robert Newman

Robert Newman is a novelist, performer, & musician. His latest latest show is a the genre-busting musical *No Planet B- The History Of The World Backwards*. His third novel, *The Fountain At The Centre Of The World,* has been published in five countries.

## Mark Watson

Mark Watson, a stand up comedian, has been nominated for the Perrier newcomer, Barry, Time Out & South Bank Awards in the last twelve months. He didn't win any of them. He's performed the longest show in history, and has also published a book, *Bullet Points.*

## Adam Buxton

Adam Buxton is best known for his charity work with television in the late 90's when he helped organise programmes which encouraged disabled channels to have fun whilst thinking for themselves and building self respect. The programmes failed and Buxton was forced to become a rent boy and poet.

## Tony Law

Tony Law Yak fighter pilot. Invented the nail and has feet. Poorly educated though tries hard. Able to travel through time and hence has a very good overall grasp of history.

## Simon Munnery

Born in Edgware, raised in Watford, died all over the place.

## Andy Zaltzman

Andy is one of Britain's least marketable stand up comedians & joint creator, writer, & star of Radio 4's *The Department*, & *Political Animal*.

## Robin Ince

Robin won a poetry prize aged 9 for a stunning piece about autumn, however his prodigal moment was soon gone. He has since established *The Robin Ince Book Club*, which is a celebration of the written word, and recently won a Time Out award for outstanding achievement in comedy.

## Russell Brand

Russell is a stand up comic, tv presenter, actor, writer, radio presenter & tabloid dream.

## Andrew Maxwell

Andrew Maxwell is a multi-award winning stand up comic. He has performed all over the world, including Las Vegas where he shared a shower with James Gandolfini.

## Dan Antopolski

Is an award winning stand up comic. He recently appeared in the BBC's *Hyperdrive*, & block busting Ron Howard epic *The Da Vinci Code*, as Jesus. For about a second.

## Paul Foot

Raised in a village in the shire of Buckingham, Paul entered showbusiness by mistake following a misunderstanding at a church fete. His first appearance was as the first half of a shire horse, within the cart display team.

## Josie Long

Josie Long is a dork who likes cartoons and Scottish indie bands. She hadn't written a poem since she was a teenager until she wrote this one.

## Owen O'Neill

Owen's mother gave birth to sixteen children and was never beaten at hop-scotch. He is a comedian, actor, & proper poet.

# & The people who put it together are

### Simon Pearce
Simon is 24 & lives in London. His hobbies & interests extend from comedy, right through to poetry. He runs the Sunday Special at Up the Creek comedy club in Greenwich.

### David Shrigley
David Shrigley is an artist who makes drawings and films and stuff. He lives in Glasgow.

www.davidshrigley.com

### Lydia Thompson
Lydia Thompson is 25 and lives in Madrid. She graduated from Goldsmiths College in 2003. She currently makes illustrations and short animated films.

www.thestomachroom.co.uk

### Martin Robinson (editorial assistant)
Martin Robinson is editorial director at tall-lighthouse, a London based poetry publishing house.

www.tall-lighthouse.co.uk

# Acknowledgements

There is not a name on the previous four pages that I am not hugely indebted to, I had five weeks to get this prepared in time for the Fringe and thus had to turn my hand to some very aggressive nagging. None of the comics have received any money for this and many have had their own Edinburgh/TV/Radio shows to worry about, this only compounds my gratitude.

Apologies to Russell Brand, Mark Watson, and Boothby Graffoe who were harassed for poetry to the point whereby their options narrowed to; write me a poem, take civil action, or beat me up. Thank goodness they all chose the former.

Thanks to Tim Key, Arthur Smith, and Simon Munnery for being so enthusiastic and helpful. & indulge me as I heap yet more thanks onto Mr Munnery who solved the foreword conundrum with deft aplomb.

David Shrigley for being so helpful to someone he's never heard of let alone met. My good friend Lydia Thompson for giving up so much time and tolerating my incessant- again- nagging.

Martin Robinson for his encouragement, and help putting this together.

And lastly the following amazing friends and family who lent me money to publish this book; Charlie March, James Hoare, Leo Goddard, Ed Coleman, and my Mum & Dad. None of whom are wealthy and none of whom expect a profit on their investment.

Which is fortunate really.

It's been marvellous fun.

Simon.

www.lookatyou.info